Fictional Character Building Workbook

By April Thomas

Printed in the United States of America

First Printing, 2016

Ascension Artists Group LLC

www.IAM2911.com

Hello, my name is April Thomas, and I am a young adult fiction author. I stand for believing in your destiny, achieving your dreams by not allowing life's obstacles to stop you from reaching the top of your mountain. In life, I have been through many painful tragedies and I have learned the best way to handle it, is to go through it and raise above. Don't stop working towards your Destiny.

Over the past six years I have written and published twelve fictional books on stories of empowerment, endurance, and victory over darkness. I believe we all have a destiny a purpose for being here, and when we don't live up to our destiny we not only rob ourselves we rob each other of what we were sent here to do, to improve the lives of everyone.

My first book is Endurance The Power Within, It's a story of overcoming obstacles and not allowing the negative things of life to stop us. I write these books to inspire, entertain, and motivate people into being their true self.

I look forward to getting to know my readers and learning more about you and how you overcame or are overcoming life's challenges so that you can live your destiny. Please reach out to me anytime through Facebook or Twitter, and if you have read any of my books I would love for you to share your thoughts through a review. Have a wonderful day and live the life you were meant to live.

Welcome and thank you for purchasing my Fictional Character Building Workbook. The Purpose of this workbook is to help with developing a character who appears very real to the reader, so real that the reader feels as if the character will walk right into their real world. Creating fictional characters for me is a lot of fun just as much fun as creating the world that they live in.

How to use the workbook:
Fill in the blanks concerning the characters basics and personality. Answer the following questions concerning the character and your done. Having all of this information in one place is very helpful when working on your books.

The end results of this workbook is to hone in on your craft and have fun. I hope that you enjoy this workbook, and it helps you to organize your thoughts and concepts for the unique characters you are creating.

Book_____ Series_____ Protagonist or Antagonists

Full Name_____

D.O.B_____ Age _____ Nationality_____

Home Town or City _____ State or Country_____

Astrological sign_____ Religion_____ Beliefs_____

Married__ Single__ _What celebrity does this character most resemble_____

Human__ Alien__ Dimensional being___ Animal____

Offspring_____ How many____

What is this character's mind set_____
_____
_____
_____

Immediate Family Members.
Mother_____ Nationality _____ Religion _____ D.O.B ____
Father_____ Nationality_____ Religion _____ D.O.B ____
Brothers_____, _____, _____

Sisters _____, _____, _____

Additional notes about this character:_____
_____
_____
_____
_____
_____
_____
_____
_____
_____
_____
_____
_____
_____
_____
_____
_____
_____

Extended Family Members: Uncles & Aunts _____

Cousins_____Grand Parents_____
_____   _____

Book_____ Series_____ Protagonist or Antagonists

Full Name_____

D.O.B_____ Age _____ Nationality_____

Home Town or City _____ State or Country_____

Astrological sign_____ Religion_____ Beliefs_____

Married__ Single__ _What celebrity does this character most resemble_____

Human__ Alien__ Dimensional being___ Animal_____

Offspring_____ How many_____

What is this character's mind set_____
_____
_____
_____

Immediate Family Members.
Mother_____ Nationality _____ Religion _____ D.O.B ____
Father_____ Nationality_____ Religion _____ D.O.B ____
Brothers_____, _____, _____

Sisters _____, _____, _____

Additional notes about this character:_____
_____
_____
_____
_____
_____
_____
_____
_____
_____
_____
_____
_____
_____
_____
_____
_____
_____

Extended Family Members: Uncles & Aunts _____

Cousins_____Grand Parents_____
_____   _____

Book_____ Series_____ Protagonist or Antagonists

Full Name_____

D.O.B_____ Age _____ Nationality_____

Home Town or City _____ State or Country_____

Astrological sign_____ Religion_____ Beliefs_____

Married__ Single__ _What celebrity does this character most resemble_____

Human__ Alien__ Dimensional being___ Animal____

Offspring_____ How many____

What is this character's mind set_____
_____
_____
_____

Immediate Family Members.
Mother_____ Nationality _____ Religion _____ D.O.B ____
Father_____ Nationality_____ Religion _____ D.O.B ____
Brothers_____, _____, _____

Sisters _____, _____, _____

Additional notes about this character:_____
_____
_____
_____
_____
_____
_____
_____
_____
_____
_____
_____
_____
_____
_____
_____
_____
_____

Extended Family Members: Uncles & Aunts _____

Cousins_____Grand Parents_____
_____   _____

Book_____ Series_____ Protagonist or Antagonists

Full Name_____

D.O.B_____ Age _____ Nationality_____

Home Town or City _____ State or Country_____

Astrological sign_____ Religion_____ Beliefs_____

Married__ Single__ _What celebrity does this character most resemble_____

Human__ Alien__ Dimensional being___ Animal_____

Offspring_____ How many_____

What is this character's mind set_____
_____
_____
_____

Immediate Family Members.
Mother_____ Nationality _____ Religion _____ D.O.B ____
Father_____ Nationality_____ Religion _____ D.O.B ____
Brothers_____, _____, _____

Sisters _____, _____, _____

Additional notes about this character:_____
_____
_____
_____
_____
_____
_____
_____
_____
_____
_____
_____
_____
_____
_____
_____
_____
_____

Extended Family Members: Uncles & Aunts _____

Cousins_____Grand Parents_____
_____   _____

Book_____ Series_____ Protagonist or Antagonists

Full Name_____

D.O.B_____ Age _____ Nationality_____

Home Town or City _____ State or Country_____

Astrological sign_____ Religion_____ Beliefs_____

Married__ Single__ _What celebrity does this character most resemble_____

Human__ Alien__ Dimensional being___ Animal____

Offspring_____ How many____

What is this character's mind set_____
_____
_____
_____

Immediate Family Members.
Mother_____ Nationality _____ Religion _____ D.O.B ____
Father_____ Nationality_____ Religion _____ D.O.B ____
Brothers_____, _____, _____

Sisters _____, _____, _____

Additional notes about this character:_____
_____
_____
_____
_____
_____
_____
_____
_____
_____
_____
_____
_____
_____
_____
_____
_____

Extended Family Members: Uncles & Aunts _____

Cousins_____Grand Parents_____
_____   _____

Book_____ Series_____ Protagonist or Antagonists

Full Name_____

D.O.B_____ Age _____ Nationality_____

Home Town or City _____ State or Country_____

Astrological sign_____ Religion_____ Beliefs_____

Married__ Single__ _What celebrity does this character most resemble_____

Human__ Alien__ Dimensional being___ Animal____

Offspring_____ How many____

What is this character's mind set_____
_____
_____
_____

Immediate Family Members.
Mother_____ Nationality _____ Religion _____ D.O.B ____
Father_____ Nationality_____ Religion _____ D.O.B ____
Brothers_____, _____, _____

Sisters _____, _____, _____

Additional notes about this character:_____
_____
_____
_____
_____
_____
_____
_____
_____
_____
_____
_____
_____
_____
_____
_____
_____
_____
_____

Extended Family Members: Uncles & Aunts _____

Cousins_____Grand Parents_____
_____   _____

Book_____ Series_____ Protagonist or Antagonists

Full Name_____

D.O.B_____ Age _____ Nationality_____

Home Town or City _____ State or Country_____

Astrological sign_____ Religion_____ Beliefs_____

Married__ Single__ .What celebrity does this character most resemble_____

Human__ Alien__ Dimensional being___ Animal_____

Offspring_____ How many_____

What is this character's mind set_____
_____
_____
_____

Immediate Family Members.
Mother_____ Nationality _____ Religion _____ D.O.B _____
Father_____ Nationality_____ Religion _____ D.O.B _____
Brothers_____, _____, _____

Sisters _____, _____, _____

Additional notes about this character:_____
_____
_____
_____
_____
_____
_____
_____
_____
_____
_____
_____
_____
_____
_____
_____
_____

Extended Family Members: Uncles & Aunts _____

Cousins_____Grand Parents_____
_____   _____

Book_____ Series_____ Protagonist or Antagonists

Full Name_____

D.O.B_____ Age _____ Nationality_____

Home Town or City _____ State or Country_____

Astrological sign_____ Religion_____ Beliefs_____

Married__ Single___ _What celebrity does this character most resemble_____

Human__ Alien__ Dimensional being___ Animal_____

Offspring_____ How many_____

What is this character's mind set_____
_____
_____
_____

Immediate Family Members.
Mother_____ Nationality _____ Religion _____ D.O.B ____
Father_____ Nationality_____ Religion _____ D.O.B ____
Brothers_____, _____, _____

Sisters _____, _____, _____

Additional notes about this character:_____
_____
_____
_____
_____
_____
_____
_____
_____
_____
_____
_____
_____
_____
_____
_____
_____
_____

Extended Family Members: Uncles & Aunts _____

Cousins_____Grand Parents_____
_____   _____

Book_____ Series_____ Protagonist or Antagonists

Full Name_____

D.O.B_____ Age _____ Nationality_____

Home Town or City _____ State or Country_____

Astrological sign_____ Religion_____ Beliefs_____

Married__ Single__ .What celebrity does this character most resemble_____

Human__ Alien__ Dimensional being___ Animal____

Offspring_____ How many____

What is this character's mind set_____
_____
_____
_____

Immediate Family Members.
Mother_____ Nationality _____ Religion _____ D.O.B ____
Father_____ Nationality_____ Religion _____ D.O.B ____
Brothers_____, _____, _____

Sisters _____, _____, _____

Additional notes about this character:_____
_____
_____
_____
_____
_____
_____
_____
_____
_____
_____
_____
_____
_____
_____
_____
_____

Extended Family Members: Uncles & Aunts _____

Cousins_____Grand Parents_____
_____   _____

Book_____ Series_____ Protagonist or Antagonists

Full Name_____

D.O.B_____ Age _____ Nationality_____

Home Town or City _____ State or Country_____

Astrological sign_____ Religion_____ Beliefs_____

Married__ Single__ .What celebrity does this character most resemble_____

Human__ Alien__ Dimensional being___ Animal____

Offspring_____ How many____

What is this character's mind set_____
_____
_____
_____

Immediate Family Members.
Mother_____ Nationality _____ Religion _____ D.O.B ____
Father_____ Nationality_____ Religion _____ D.O.B ____
Brothers_____, _____, _____

Sisters _____, _____, _____

Additional notes about this character:_____
_____
_____
_____
_____
_____
_____
_____
_____
_____
_____
_____
_____
_____
_____
_____
_____
_____

Extended Family Members: Uncles & Aunts _____

Cousins_____Grand Parents_____
_____   _____

Book_____ Series_____ Protagonist or Antagonists

Full Name_____

D.O.B_____ Age _____ Nationality_____

Home Town or City _____ State or Country_____

Astrological sign_____ Religion_____ Beliefs_____

Married__ Single__ What celebrity does this character most resemble_____

Human__ Alien__ Dimensional being___ Animal____

Offspring_____ How many____

What is this character's mind set_____
_____
_____
_____

Immediate Family Members.
Mother_____ Nationality _____ Religion _____ D.O.B ____
Father_____ Nationality_____ Religion _____ D.O.B ____
Brothers_____, _____, _____

Sisters _____, _____, _____

Additional notes about this character:_____
_____
_____
_____
_____
_____
_____
_____
_____
_____
_____
_____
_____
_____
_____
_____
_____

Extended Family Members: Uncles & Aunts _____

Cousins_____Grand Parents_____
_____   _____

Book_____ Series_____ Protagonist or Antagonists

Full Name_____

D.O.B_____ Age _____ Nationality_____

Home Town or City _____ State or Country_____

Astrological sign_____ Religion_____ Beliefs_____

Married__ Single__ _What celebrity does this character most resemble_____

Human__ Alien__ Dimensional being___ Animal_____

Offspring_____ How many_____

What is this character's mind set_____
_____
_____
_____

Immediate Family Members.
Mother_____ Nationality _____ Religion _____ D.O.B ____
Father_____ Nationality_____ Religion _____ D.O.B ____
Brothers_____, _____, _____

Sisters _____, _____, _____

Additional notes about this character:_____
_____
_____
_____
_____
_____
_____
_____
_____
_____
_____
_____
_____
_____
_____
_____
_____
_____

Extended Family Members: Uncles & Aunts _____

Cousins_____Grand Parents_____
_____   _____

Book_____ Series_____ Protagonist or Antagonists

Full Name_____

D.O.B_____ Age _____ Nationality_____

Home Town or City _____ State or Country_____

Astrological sign_____ Religion_____ Beliefs_____

Married__ Single__ _What celebrity does this character most resemble_____

Human__ Alien__ Dimensional being____ Animal_____

Offspring_____ How many_____

What is this character's mind set_____
_____
_____
_____

Immediate Family Members.
Mother_____ Nationality _____ Religion _____ D.O.B ____
Father_____ Nationality_____ Religion _____ D.O.B ____
Brothers_____, _____, _____

Sisters _____, _____, _____

Additional notes about this character:_____
_____
_____
_____
_____
_____
_____
_____
_____
_____
_____
_____
_____
_____
_____
_____

Extended Family Members: Uncles & Aunts _____

Cousins_____Grand Parents_____
_____   _____

Book_____ Series_____ Protagonist or Antagonists

Full Name_____

D.O.B_____ Age _____ Nationality_____

Home Town or City _____ State or Country_____

Astrological sign_____ Religion_____ Beliefs_____

Married__ Single__ _What celebrity does this character most resemble_____

Human__ Alien__ Dimensional being___ Animal____

Offspring_____ How many____

What is this character's mind set_____
_____
_____
_____

Immediate Family Members.
Mother_____ Nationality _____ Religion _____ D.O.B ____
Father_____ Nationality_____ Religion _____ D.O.B ____
Brothers_____, _____, _____

Sisters _____, _____, _____

Additional notes about this character:_____
_____
_____
_____
_____
_____
_____
_____
_____
_____
_____
_____
_____
_____
_____
_____
_____
_____

Extended Family Members: Uncles & Aunts _____

Cousins_____Grand Parents_____
_____   _____

Book_____ Series_____ Protagonist or Antagonists

Full Name_____

D.O.B_____ Age _____ Nationality_____

Home Town or City _____ State or Country_____

Astrological sign_____ Religion_____ Beliefs_____

Married__ Single__ _What celebrity does this character most resemble_____

Human__ Alien__ Dimensional being____ Animal_____

Offspring_____ How many_____

What is this character's mind set_____
_____
_____
_____

Immediate Family Members.
Mother_____ Nationality _____ Religion _____ D.O.B ____
Father_____ Nationality_____ Religion _____ D.O.B ____
Brothers_____, _____, _____

Sisters _____, _____, _____

Additional notes about this character:_____
_____
_____
_____
_____
_____
_____
_____
_____
_____
_____
_____
_____
_____
_____
_____
_____

Extended Family Members: Uncles & Aunts _____

Cousins_____Grand Parents_____
_____   _____

Book_____ Series_____ Protagonist or Antagonists

Full Name_____

D.O.B_____ Age _____ Nationality_____

Home Town or City _____ State or Country_____

Astrological sign_____ Religion_____ Beliefs_____

Married__ Single__ _What celebrity does this character most resemble_____

Human__ Alien__ Dimensional being___ Animal____

Offspring_____ How many____

What is this character's mind set_____
_____
_____
_____

Immediate Family Members.
Mother_____ Nationality _____ Religion _____ D.O.B ____
Father_____ Nationality_____ Religion _____ D.O.B ____
Brothers_____, _____, _____

Sisters _____, _____, _____

Additional notes about this character:_____
_____
_____
_____
_____
_____
_____
_____
_____
_____
_____
_____
_____
_____
_____
_____
_____
_____

Extended Family Members: Uncles & Aunts _____

Cousins_____Grand Parents_____
_____   _____

Book_____ Series_____ Protagonist or Antagonists

Full Name_____

D.O.B_____ Age _____ Nationality_____

Home Town or City _____ State or Country_____

Astrological sign_____ Religion_____ Beliefs_____

Married__ Single__ _What celebrity does this character most resemble_____

Human__ Alien__ Dimensional being___ Animal_____

Offspring_____ How many____

What is this character's mind set_____
_____
_____
_____

Immediate Family Members.
Mother_____ Nationality _____ Religion _____ D.O.B ____
Father_____ Nationality_____ Religion _____ D.O.B ____
Brothers_____, _____, _____

Sisters _____, _____, _____

Additional notes about this character:_____
_____
_____
_____
_____
_____
_____
_____
_____
_____
_____
_____
_____
_____
_____
_____
_____

Extended Family Members: Uncles & Aunts _____

Cousins_____Grand Parents_____
_____   _____

Book_____ Series_____ Protagonist or Antagonists

Full Name_____

D.O.B_____ Age _____ Nationality_____

Home Town or City _____ State or Country_____

Astrological sign_____ Religion_____ Beliefs_____

Married__ Single__ .What celebrity does this character most resemble_____

Human__ Alien__ Dimensional being___ Animal_____

Offspring_____ How many_____

What is this character's mind set_____
_____
_____
_____

Immediate Family Members.
Mother_____ Nationality _____ Religion _____ D.O.B ____
Father_____ Nationality_____ Religion _____ D.O.B ____
Brothers_____, _____, _____

Sisters _____, _____, _____

Additional notes about this character:_____
_____
_____
_____
_____
_____
_____
_____
_____
_____
_____
_____
_____
_____
_____
_____
_____

Extended Family Members: Uncles & Aunts _____

Cousins_____Grand Parents_____
_____   _____

Book_____ Series_____ Protagonist or Antagonists

Full Name_____

D.O.B_____ Age _____ Nationality_____

Home Town or City _____ State or Country_____

Astrological sign_____ Religion_____ Beliefs_____

Married__ Single__ _What celebrity does this character most resemble_____

Human__ Alien__ Dimensional being___ Animal____

Offspring_____ How many____

What is this character's mind set_____
_____
_____
_____

Immediate Family Members.
Mother_____ Nationality _____ Religion _____ D.O.B ____
Father_____ Nationality_____ Religion _____ D.O.B ____
Brothers_____, _____, _____

Sisters _____, _____, _____

Additional notes about this character:_____
_____
_____
_____
_____
_____
_____
_____
_____
_____
_____
_____
_____
_____
_____
_____
_____
_____

Extended Family Members: Uncles & Aunts _____

Cousins_____Grand Parents_____
_____   _____

Book_____ Series_____ Protagonist or Antagonists

Full Name_____

D.O.B_____ Age _____ Nationality_____

Home Town or City _____ State or Country_____

Astrological sign_____ Religion_____ Beliefs_____

Married__ Single__ .What celebrity does this character most resemble_____

Human__ Alien__ Dimensional being___ Animal_____

Offspring_____ How many_____

What is this character's mind set_____
_____
_____
_____

Immediate Family Members.
Mother_____ Nationality _____ Religion _____ D.O.B ____
Father_____ Nationality_____ Religion _____ D.O.B ____
Brothers_____, _____, _____

Sisters _____, _____, _____

Additional notes about this character:_____
_____
_____
_____
_____
_____
_____
_____
_____
_____
_____
_____
_____
_____
_____
_____
_____
_____
_____

Extended Family Members: Uncles & Aunts _____

Cousins_____Grand Parents_____
_____   _____

Book_____ Series_____ Protagonist or Antagonists

Full Name_____

D.O.B_____ Age _____ Nationality_____

Home Town or City _____ State or Country_____

Astrological sign_____ Religion_____ Beliefs_____

Married__ Single__ .What celebrity does this character most resemble_____

Human__ Alien__ Dimensional being___ Animal____

Offspring_____ How many____

What is this character's mind set_____
_____
_____
_____

Immediate Family Members.
Mother_____ Nationality _____ Religion _____ D.O.B ____
Father_____ Nationality_____ Religion _____ D.O.B ____
Brothers_____, _____, _____

Sisters _____, _____, _____

Additional notes about this character:_____
_____
_____
_____
_____
_____
_____
_____
_____
_____
_____
_____
_____
_____
_____
_____
_____

Extended Family Members: Uncles & Aunts _____

Cousins_____Grand Parents_____
_____   _____

Book_____ Series_____ Protagonist or Antagonists

Full Name_____

D.O.B_____ Age _____ Nationality_____

Home Town or City _____ State or Country_____

Astrological sign_____ Religion_____ Beliefs_____

Married__ Single__ _What celebrity does this character most resemble_____

Human__ Alien__ Dimensional being___ Animal____

Offspring_____ How many____

What is this character's mind set_____
_____
_____
_____

Immediate Family Members.
Mother_____ Nationality _____ Religion _____ D.O.B ____
Father_____ Nationality_____ Religion _____ D.O.B ____
Brothers_____, _____, _____

Sisters _____, _____, _____

Additional notes about this character:_____
_____
_____
_____
_____
_____
_____
_____
_____
_____
_____
_____
_____
_____
_____
_____

Extended Family Members: Uncles & Aunts _____

Cousins_____Grand Parents_____
_____   _____

Book_____ Series_____ Protagonist or Antagonists

Full Name_____

D.O.B_____ Age _____ Nationality_____

Home Town or City _____ State or Country_____

Astrological sign_____ Religion_____ Beliefs_____

Married___ Single___ _What celebrity does this character most resemble_____

Human___ Alien___ Dimensional being____ Animal_____

Offspring_____ How many_____

What is this character's mind set_____
_____
_____
_____

Immediate Family Members.
Mother_____ Nationality _____ Religion _____ D.O.B ____
Father_____ Nationality_____ Religion _____ D.O.B ____
Brothers_____, _____, _____

Sisters _____, _____, _____

Additional notes about this character:_____
_____
_____
_____
_____
_____
_____
_____
_____
_____
_____
_____
_____
_____
_____
_____
_____
_____

Extended Family Members: Uncles & Aunts _____

Cousins_____Grand Parents_____
_____   _____

Book_____ Series_____ Protagonist or Antagonists

Full Name_____

D.O.B_____ Age _____ Nationality_____

Home Town or City _____ State or Country_____

Astrological sign_____ Religion_____ Beliefs_____

Married__ Single__ _What celebrity does this character most resemble_____

Human__ Alien__ Dimensional being___ Animal_____

Offspring_____ How many_____

What is this character's mind set_____
_____
_____
_____

Immediate Family Members.
Mother_____ Nationality _____ Religion _____ D.O.B ____
Father_____ Nationality_____ Religion _____ D.O.B ____
Brothers_____, _____, _____

Sisters _____, _____, _____

Additional notes about this character:_____
_____
_____
_____
_____
_____
_____
_____
_____
_____
_____
_____
_____
_____
_____
_____
_____
_____
_____

Extended Family Members: Uncles & Aunts _____

Cousins_____Grand Parents_____
_____   _____

Book_____ Series_____ Protagonist or Antagonists

Full Name_____

D.O.B_____ Age _____ Nationality_____

Home Town or City _____ State or Country_____

Astrological sign_____ Religion_____ Beliefs_____

Married__ Single__ _What celebrity does this character most resemble_____

Human__ Alien__ Dimensional being___ Animal_____

Offspring_____ How many____

What is this character's mind set_____
_____
_____
_____

Immediate Family Members.
Mother_____ Nationality _____ Religion _____ D.O.B ____
Father_____ Nationality_____ Religion _____ D.O.B ____
Brothers_____, _____, _____

Sisters _____, _____, _____

Additional notes about this character:_____
_____
_____
_____
_____
_____
_____
_____
_____
_____
_____
_____
_____
_____
_____
_____
_____
_____

Extended Family Members: Uncles & Aunts _____

Cousins_____Grand Parents_____
_____   _____

Book_____ Series_____ Protagonist or Antagonists

Full Name_____

D.O.B_____ Age _____ Nationality_____

Home Town or City _____ State or Country_____

Astrological sign_____ Religion_____ Beliefs_____

Married__ Single__ _What celebrity does this character most resemble_____

Human__ Alien__ Dimensional being___ Animal_____

Offspring_____ How many_____

What is this character's mind set_____
_____
_____
_____

Immediate Family Members.
Mother_____ Nationality _____ Religion _____ D.O.B ____
Father_____ Nationality_____ Religion _____ D.O.B ____
Brothers_____, _____, _____

Sisters _____, _____, _____

Additional notes about this character:_____
_____
_____
_____
_____
_____
_____
_____
_____
_____
_____
_____
_____
_____
_____
_____
_____
_____

Extended Family Members: Uncles & Aunts _____

Cousins_____Grand Parents_____
_____   _____

Book_____ Series_____ Protagonist or Antagonists

Full Name_____

D.O.B_____ Age _____ Nationality_____

Home Town or City _____ State or Country_____

Astrological sign_____ Religion_____ Beliefs_____

Married__ Single__ _What celebrity does this character most resemble_____

Human__ Alien__ Dimensional being___ Animal____

Offspring_____ How many____

What is this character's mind set_____
_____
_____
_____

Immediate Family Members.
Mother_____ Nationality _____ Religion _____ D.O.B ____
Father_____ Nationality_____ Religion _____ D.O.B ____
Brothers_____, _____, _____

Sisters _____, _____, _____

Additional notes about this character:_____
_____
_____
_____
_____
_____
_____
_____
_____
_____
_____
_____
_____
_____
_____
_____
_____

Extended Family Members: Uncles & Aunts _____

Cousins_____Grand Parents_____
_____   _____

Book_____ Series_____ Protagonist or Antagonists

Full Name_____

D.O.B_____ Age _____ Nationality_____

Home Town or City _____ State or Country_____

Astrological sign_____ Religion_____ Beliefs_____

Married___ Single___ _What celebrity does this character most resemble_____

Human___ Alien___ Dimensional being____ Animal_____

Offspring_____ How many_____

What is this character's mind set_____
_____
_____
_____

Immediate Family Members.
Mother_____ Nationality _____ Religion _____ D.O.B ____
Father_____ Nationality_____ Religion _____ D.O.B ____
Brothers_____, _____, _____

Sisters _____, _____, _____

Additional notes about this character:_____
_____
_____
_____
_____
_____
_____
_____
_____
_____
_____
_____
_____
_____
_____
_____
_____

Extended Family Members: Uncles & Aunts _____

Cousins_____Grand Parents_____
_____   _____

Book_____ Series_____ Protagonist or Antagonists

Full Name_____

D.O.B_____ Age _____ Nationality_____

Home Town or City _____ State or Country_____

Astrological sign_____ Religion_____ Beliefs_____

Married__ Single__ _What celebrity does this character most resemble_____

Human__ Alien__ Dimensional being___ Animal_____

Offspring_____ How many_____

What is this character's mind set_____
_____
_____
_____

Immediate Family Members.
Mother_____ Nationality _____ Religion _____ D.O.B ____
Father_____ Nationality_____ Religion _____ D.O.B ____
Brothers_____, _____, _____

Sisters _____, _____, _____

Additional notes about this character:_____
_____
_____
_____
_____
_____
_____
_____
_____
_____
_____
_____
_____
_____
_____
_____
_____
_____

Extended Family Members: Uncles & Aunts _____

Cousins_____Grand Parents_____
_____   _____

Book_____ Series_____ Protagonist or Antagonists

Full Name_____

D.O.B_____ Age _____ Nationality_____

Home Town or City _____ State or Country_____

Astrological sign_____ Religion_____ Beliefs_____

Married__ Single__ _What celebrity does this character most resemble_____

Human__ Alien__ Dimensional being___ Animal_____

Offspring_____ How many_____

What is this character's mind set_____
_____
_____
_____

Immediate Family Members.
Mother_____ Nationality _____ Religion _____ D.O.B _____
Father_____ Nationality_____ Religion _____ D.O.B _____
Brothers_____, _____, _____

Sisters _____, _____, _____

Additional notes about this character:_____
_____
_____
_____
_____
_____
_____
_____
_____
_____
_____
_____
_____
_____
_____
_____
_____
_____

Extended Family Members: Uncles & Aunts _____

Cousins_____Grand Parents_____
_____   _____

Book_____ Series_____ Protagonist or Antagonists

Full Name_____

D.O.B_____ Age _____ Nationality_____

Home Town or City _____ State or Country_____

Astrological sign_____ Religion_____ Beliefs_____

Married__ Single__ _What celebrity does this character most resemble_____

Human__ Alien__ Dimensional being___ Animal____

Offspring_____ How many____

What is this character's mind set_____
_____
_____
_____

Immediate Family Members.
Mother_____ Nationality _____ Religion _____ D.O.B ____
Father_____ Nationality_____ Religion _____ D.O.B ____
Brothers_____, _____, _____

Sisters _____, _____, _____

Additional notes about this character:_____
_____
_____
_____
_____
_____
_____
_____
_____
_____
_____
_____
_____
_____
_____
_____
_____

Extended Family Members: Uncles & Aunts _____

Cousins_____Grand Parents_____
_____   _____

Book_____ Series_____ Protagonist or Antagonists

Full Name_____

D.O.B_____ Age _____ Nationality_____

Home Town or City _____ State or Country_____

Astrological sign_____ Religion_____ Beliefs_____

Married__ Single__ .What celebrity does this character most resemble_____

Human__ Alien__ Dimensional being___ Animal____

Offspring_____ How many____

What is this character's mind set_____
_____
_____
_____

Immediate Family Members.
Mother_____ Nationality _____ Religion _____ D.O.B ____
Father_____ Nationality_____ Religion _____ D.O.B ____
Brothers_____, _____, _____

Sisters _____, _____, _____

Additional notes about this character:_____
_____
_____
_____
_____
_____
_____
_____
_____
_____
_____
_____
_____
_____
_____
_____
_____

Extended Family Members: Uncles & Aunts _____

Cousins_____Grand Parents_____
_____   _____

Book_____ Series_____ Protagonist or Antagonists

Full Name_____

D.O.B_____ Age _____ Nationality_____

Home Town or City _____ State or Country_____

Astrological sign_____ Religion_____ Beliefs_____

Married__ Single__ _What celebrity does this character most resemble_____

Human__ Alien__ Dimensional being___ Animal____

Offspring_____ How many____

What is this character's mind set_____
_____
_____
_____

Immediate Family Members.
Mother_____ Nationality _____ Religion _____ D.O.B ____
Father_____ Nationality_____ Religion _____ D.O.B ____
Brothers_____, _____, _____

Sisters _____, _____, _____

Additional notes about this character:_____
_____
_____
_____
_____
_____
_____
_____
_____
_____
_____
_____
_____
_____
_____
_____
_____
_____
_____

Extended Family Members: Uncles & Aunts _____

Cousins_____Grand Parents_____
_____   _____

Book_____ Series_____ Protagonist or Antagonists

Full Name_____

D.O.B_____ Age _____ Nationality_____

Home Town or City _____ State or Country_____

Astrological sign_____ Religion_____ Beliefs_____

Married__ Single__ .What celebrity does this character most resemble_____

Human__ Alien__ Dimensional being___ Animal____

Offspring_____ How many____

What is this character's mind set_____
_____
_____
_____

Immediate Family Members.
Mother_____ Nationality _____ Religion _____ D.O.B ____
Father_____ Nationality_____ Religion _____ D.O.B ____
Brothers_____, _____, _____

Sisters _____, _____, _____

Additional notes about this character:_____
_____
_____
_____
_____
_____
_____
_____
_____
_____
_____
_____
_____
_____
_____
_____
_____
_____

Extended Family Members: Uncles & Aunts _____

Cousins_____Grand Parents_____
_____   _____

Book_____ Series_____ Protagonist or Antagonists

Full Name_____

D.O.B_____ Age _____ Nationality_____

Home Town or City _____ State or Country_____

Astrological sign_____ Religion_____ Beliefs_____

Married__ Single___ .What celebrity does this character most resemble_____

Human__ Alien__ Dimensional being___ Animal_____

Offspring_____ How many_____

What is this character's mind set_____
_____
_____
_____

Immediate Family Members.
Mother_____ Nationality _____ Religion _____ D.O.B ____
Father_____ Nationality_____ Religion _____ D.O.B ____
Brothers_____, _____, _____

Sisters _____, _____, _____

Additional notes about this character:_____
_____
_____
_____
_____
_____
_____
_____
_____
_____
_____
_____
_____
_____
_____
_____
_____

Extended Family Members: Uncles & Aunts _____

Cousins_____Grand Parents_____
_____   _____

Book_____ Series_____ Protagonist or Antagonists

Full Name_____

D.O.B_____ Age _____ Nationality_____

Home Town or City _____ State or Country_____

Astrological sign_____ Religion_____ Beliefs_____

Married__ Single__ _What celebrity does this character most resemble_____

Human__ Alien__ Dimensional being___ Animal_____

Offspring_____ How many_____

What is this character's mind set_____
_____
_____
_____

Immediate Family Members.
Mother_____ Nationality _____ Religion _____ D.O.B ____
Father_____ Nationality_____ Religion _____ D.O.B ____
Brothers_____, _____, _____

Sisters _____, _____, _____

Additional notes about this character:_____
_____
_____
_____
_____
_____
_____
_____
_____
_____
_____
_____
_____
_____
_____
_____
_____
_____

Extended Family Members: Uncles & Aunts _____

Cousins_____Grand Parents_____
_____   _____

Book_____ Series_____ Protagonist or Antagonists

Full Name_____

D.O.B_____ Age _____ Nationality_____

Home Town or City _____ State or Country_____

Astrological sign_____ Religion_____ Beliefs_____

Married__ Single__ _What celebrity does this character most resemble_____

Human__ Alien__ Dimensional being___ Animal_____

Offspring_____ How many_____

What is this character's mind set_____
_____
_____
_____

Immediate Family Members.
Mother_____ Nationality _____ Religion _____ D.O.B ____
Father_____ Nationality_____ Religion _____ D.O.B ____
Brothers_____, _____, _____

Sisters _____, _____, _____

Additional notes about this character:_____
_____
_____
_____
_____
_____
_____
_____
_____
_____
_____
_____
_____
_____
_____
_____
_____

Extended Family Members: Uncles & Aunts _____

Cousins_____Grand Parents_____
_____   _____

Book_____ Series_____ Protagonist or Antagonists

Full Name_____

D.O.B_____ Age _____ Nationality_____

Home Town or City _____ State or Country_____

Astrological sign_____ Religion_____ Beliefs_____

Married__ Single__ _What celebrity does this character most resemble_____

Human__ Alien__ Dimensional being___ Animal_____

Offspring_____ How many_____

What is this character's mind set_____
_____
_____
_____

Immediate Family Members.
Mother_____ Nationality _____ Religion _____ D.O.B ____
Father_____ Nationality_____ Religion _____ D.O.B ____
Brothers_____, _____, _____

Sisters _____, _____, _____

Additional notes about this character:_____
_____
_____
_____
_____
_____
_____
_____
_____
_____
_____
_____
_____
_____
_____
_____
_____
_____

Extended Family Members: Uncles & Aunts _____

Cousins_____Grand Parents_____
_____   _____

Book_____ Series_____ Protagonist or Antagonists

Full Name_____

D.O.B_____ Age _____ Nationality_____

Home Town or City _____ State or Country_____

Astrological sign_____ Religion_____ Beliefs_____

Married___ Single___ _What celebrity does this character most resemble_____

Human___ Alien___ Dimensional being____ Animal_____

Offspring_____ How many_____

What is this character's mind set_____
_____
_____
_____

Immediate Family Members.
Mother_____ Nationality _____ Religion _____ D.O.B ____
Father_____ Nationality_____ Religion _____ D.O.B ____
Brothers_____, _____, _____

Sisters _____, _____, _____

Additional notes about this character:_____
_____
_____
_____
_____
_____
_____
_____
_____
_____
_____
_____
_____
_____
_____
_____
_____

Extended Family Members: Uncles & Aunts _____

Cousins_____Grand Parents_____
_____   _____

Book_____ Series_____ Protagonist or Antagonists

Full Name_____

D.O.B_____ Age _____ Nationality_____

Home Town or City _____ State or Country_____

Astrological sign_____ Religion_____ Beliefs_____

Married__ Single__ .What celebrity does this character most resemble_____

Human__ Alien__ Dimensional being___ Animal____

Offspring_____ How many____

What is this character's mind set_____
_____
_____
_____

Immediate Family Members.
Mother_____ Nationality _____ Religion _____ D.O.B ____
Father_____ Nationality_____ Religion _____ D.O.B ____
Brothers_____, _____, _____

Sisters _____, _____, _____

Additional notes about this character:_____
_____
_____
_____
_____
_____
_____
_____
_____
_____
_____
_____
_____
_____
_____
_____
_____
_____

Extended Family Members: Uncles & Aunts _____

Cousins_____Grand Parents_____
_____   _____

Book_____ Series_____ Protagonist or Antagonists

Full Name_____

D.O.B_____ Age _____ Nationality_____

Home Town or City _____ State or Country_____

Astrological sign_____ Religion_____ Beliefs_____

Married__ Single___ .What celebrity does this character most resemble_____

Human__ Alien__ Dimensional being___ Animal____

Offspring_____ How many____

What is this character's mind set_____
_____
_____
_____

Immediate Family Members.
Mother_____ Nationality _____ Religion _____ D.O.B ____
Father_____ Nationality_____ Religion _____ D.O.B ____
Brothers_____, _____, _____

Sisters _____, _____, _____

Additional notes about this character:_____
_____
_____
_____
_____
_____
_____
_____
_____
_____
_____
_____
_____
_____
_____
_____
_____

Extended Family Members: Uncles & Aunts _____

Cousins_____Grand Parents_____
_____   _____

Book_____ Series_____ Protagonist or Antagonists

Full Name_____

D.O.B_____ Age _____ Nationality_____

Home Town or City _____ State or Country_____

Astrological sign_____ Religion_____ Beliefs_____

Married__ Single__ _What celebrity does this character most resemble_____

Human__ Alien__ Dimensional being___ Animal____

Offspring_____ How many____

What is this character's mind set_____
_____
_____
_____

<u>Immediate Family Members.</u>
Mother_____ Nationality _____ Religion _____ D.O.B ____
Father_____ Nationality_____ Religion _____ D.O.B ____
Brothers_____, _____, _____

Sisters _____, _____, _____

Additional notes about this character:_____
_____
_____
_____
_____
_____
_____
_____
_____
_____
_____
_____
_____
_____
_____
_____
_____

Extended Family Members: Uncles & Aunts _____

Cousins_____Grand Parents_____
_____   _____

Book_____ Series_____ Protagonist or Antagonists

Full Name_____

D.O.B_____ Age _____ Nationality_____

Home Town or City _____ State or Country_____

Astrological sign_____ Religion_____ Beliefs_____

Married__ Single__ _What celebrity does this character most resemble_____

Human__ Alien__ Dimensional being___ Animal____

Offspring_____ How many____

What is this character's mind set_____
_____
_____
_____

Immediate Family Members.
Mother_____ Nationality _____ Religion _____ D.O.B ____
Father_____ Nationality_____ Religion _____ D.O.B ____
Brothers_____, _____, _____

Sisters _____, _____, _____

Additional notes about this character:_____
_____
_____
_____
_____
_____
_____
_____
_____
_____
_____
_____
_____
_____
_____
_____
_____
_____

Extended Family Members: Uncles & Aunts _____

Cousins_____Grand Parents_____
_____   _____

Book_____ Series_____ Protagonist or Antagonists

Full Name_____

D.O.B_____ Age _____ Nationality_____

Home Town or City _____ State or Country_____

Astrological sign_____ Religion_____ Beliefs_____

Married__ Single__ _What celebrity does this character most resemble_____

Human__ Alien__ Dimensional being___ Animal____

Offspring_____ How many____

What is this character's mind set_____
_____
_____
_____

Immediate Family Members.
Mother_____ Nationality _____ Religion _____ D.O.B ____
Father_____ Nationality_____ Religion _____ D.O.B ____
Brothers_____, _____, _____

Sisters _____, _____, _____

Additional notes about this character:_____
_____
_____
_____
_____
_____
_____
_____
_____
_____
_____
_____
_____
_____
_____
_____
_____
_____

Extended Family Members: Uncles & Aunts _____

Cousins_____Grand Parents_____
_____   _____

Book_____ Series_____ Protagonist or Antagonists

Full Name_____

D.O.B_____ Age _____ Nationality_____

Home Town or City _____ State or Country_____

Astrological sign_____ Religion_____ Beliefs_____

Married__ Single__ _What celebrity does this character most resemble_____

Human__ Alien__ Dimensional being___ Animal_____

Offspring_____ How many_____

What is this character's mind set_____
_____
_____
_____

Immediate Family Members.
Mother_____ Nationality _____ Religion _____ D.O.B ____
Father_____ Nationality_____ Religion _____ D.O.B ____
Brothers_____, _____, _____

Sisters _____, _____, _____

Additional notes about this character:_____
_____
_____
_____
_____
_____
_____
_____
_____
_____
_____
_____
_____
_____
_____
_____
_____
_____

Extended Family Members: Uncles & Aunts _____

Cousins_____Grand Parents_____
_____   _____

Book_____ Series_____ Protagonist or Antagonists

Full Name_____

D.O.B_____ Age _____ Nationality_____

Home Town or City _____ State or Country_____

Astrological sign_____ Religion_____ Beliefs_____

Married__ Single__ _What celebrity does this character most resemble_____

Human__ Alien__ Dimensional being___ Animal____

Offspring_____ How many____

What is this character's mind set_____
_____
_____
_____

Immediate Family Members.
Mother_____ Nationality _____ Religion _____ D.O.B ____
Father_____ Nationality_____ Religion _____ D.O.B ____
Brothers_____, _____, _____

Sisters _____, _____, _____

Additional notes about this character:_____
_____
_____
_____
_____
_____
_____
_____
_____
_____
_____
_____
_____
_____
_____
_____
_____

Extended Family Members: Uncles & Aunts _____

Cousins_____Grand Parents_____
_____   _____

Book_____ Series_____ Protagonist or Antagonists

Full Name_____

D.O.B_____ Age _____ Nationality_____

Home Town or City _____ State or Country_____

Astrological sign_____ Religion_____ Beliefs_____

Married__ Single__ _What celebrity does this character most resemble_____

Human__ Alien__ Dimensional being___ Animal____

Offspring_____ How many____

What is this character's mind set_____
_____
_____
_____

Immediate Family Members.
Mother_____ Nationality _____ Religion _____ D.O.B ____
Father_____ Nationality_____ Religion _____ D.O.B ____
Brothers_____, _____, _____

Sisters _____, _____, _____

Additional notes about this character:_____
_____
_____
_____
_____
_____
_____
_____
_____
_____
_____
_____
_____
_____
_____
_____

Extended Family Members: Uncles & Aunts _____

Cousins_____Grand Parents_____
_____   _____

Book_____ Series_____ Protagonist or Antagonists

Full Name_____

D.O.B_____ Age _____ Nationality_____

Home Town or City _____ State or Country_____

Astrological sign_____ Religion_____ Beliefs_____

Married___ Single___ _What celebrity does this character most resemble_____

Human___ Alien___ Dimensional being____ Animal_____

Offspring_____ How many_____

What is this character's mind set_____
_____
_____
_____

Immediate Family Members.
Mother_____ Nationality _____ Religion _____ D.O.B ____
Father_____ Nationality_____ Religion _____ D.O.B ____
Brothers_____, _____, _____

Sisters _____, _____, _____

Additional notes about this character:_____
_____
_____
_____
_____
_____
_____
_____
_____
_____
_____
_____
_____
_____
_____
_____
_____
_____

Extended Family Members: Uncles & Aunts _____

Cousins_____Grand Parents_____
_____   _____

Book_____ Series_____ Protagonist or Antagonists

Full Name_____

D.O.B_____ Age _____ Nationality_____

Home Town or City _____ State or Country_____

Astrological sign_____ Religion_____ Beliefs_____

Married__ Single__ _What celebrity does this character most resemble_____

Human__ Alien__ Dimensional being___ Animal____

Offspring_____ How many____

What is this character's mind set_____
_____
_____
_____

Immediate Family Members.
Mother_____ Nationality _____ Religion _____ D.O.B ____
Father_____ Nationality_____ Religion _____ D.O.B ____
Brothers_____, _____, _____

Sisters _____, _____, _____

Additional notes about this character:_____
_____
_____
_____
_____
_____
_____
_____
_____
_____
_____
_____
_____
_____
_____
_____
_____

Extended Family Members: Uncles & Aunts _____

Cousins_____Grand Parents_____
_____   _____

Book_____ Series_____ Protagonist or Antagonists

Full Name_____

D.O.B_____ Age _____ Nationality_____

Home Town or City _____ State or Country_____

Astrological sign_____ Religion_____ Beliefs_____

Married__ Single__ _What celebrity does this character most resemble_____

Human__ Alien__ Dimensional being___ Animal_____

Offspring_____ How many____

What is this character's mind set_____
_____
_____
_____

Immediate Family Members.
Mother_____ Nationality _____ Religion _____ D.O.B ____
Father_____ Nationality_____ Religion _____ D.O.B ____
Brothers_____, _____, _____

Sisters _____, _____, _____

Additional notes about this character:_____
_____
_____
_____
_____
_____
_____
_____
_____
_____
_____
_____
_____
_____
_____
_____
_____
_____

Extended Family Members: Uncles & Aunts _____

Cousins_____Grand Parents_____
_____   _____

Book_____ Series_____ Protagonist or Antagonists

Full Name_____

D.O.B_____ Age _____ Nationality_____

Home Town or City _____ State or Country_____

Astrological sign_____ Religion_____ Beliefs_____

Married__ Single__ _What celebrity does this character most resemble_____

Human__ Alien__ Dimensional being___ Animal____

Offspring_____ How many____

What is this character's mind set_____
_____
_____
_____

Immediate Family Members.
Mother_____ Nationality _____ Religion _____ D.O.B ____
Father_____ Nationality_____ Religion _____ D.O.B ____
Brothers_____, _____, _____

Sisters _____, _____, _____

Additional notes about this character:_____
_____
_____
_____
_____
_____
_____
_____
_____
_____
_____
_____
_____
_____
_____
_____

Extended Family Members: Uncles & Aunts _____

Cousins_____Grand Parents_____
_____   _____

Book_____ Series_____ Protagonist or Antagonists

Full Name_____

D.O.B_____ Age _____ Nationality_____

Home Town or City _____ State or Country_____

Astrological sign_____ Religion_____ Beliefs_____

Married__ Single__ _What celebrity does this character most resemble_____

Human__ Alien__ Dimensional being____ Animal_____

Offspring_____ How many_____

What is this character's mind set_____
_____
_____
_____

Immediate Family Members.
Mother_____ Nationality _____ Religion _____ D.O.B ____
Father_____ Nationality_____ Religion _____ D.O.B ____
Brothers_____, _____, _____

Sisters _____, _____, _____

Additional notes about this character:_____
_____
_____
_____
_____
_____
_____
_____
_____
_____
_____
_____
_____
_____
_____
_____
_____
_____

Extended Family Members: Uncles & Aunts _____

Cousins_____Grand Parents_____
_____   _____

Book_____ Series_____ Protagonist or Antagonists

Full Name_____

D.O.B_____ Age _____ Nationality_____

Home Town or City _____ State or Country_____

Astrological sign_____ Religion_____ Beliefs_____

Married__ Single__ _What celebrity does this character most resemble_____

Human__ Alien__ Dimensional being___ Animal____

Offspring_____ How many____

What is this character's mind set_____
_____
_____
_____

Immediate Family Members.
Mother_____ Nationality _____ Religion _____ D.O.B ____
Father_____ Nationality_____ Religion _____ D.O.B ____
Brothers_____, _____, _____

Sisters _____, _____, _____

Additional notes about this character:_____
_____
_____
_____
_____
_____
_____
_____
_____
_____
_____
_____
_____
_____
_____
_____

Extended Family Members: Uncles & Aunts _____

Cousins_____Grand Parents_____
_____   _____

Book_____ Series_____ Protagonist or Antagonists

Full Name_____

D.O.B_____ Age _____ Nationality_____

Home Town or City _____ State or Country_____

Astrological sign_____ Religion_____ Beliefs_____

Married__ Single__ _What celebrity does this character most resemble_____

Human__ Alien__ Dimensional being___ Animal____

Offspring_____ How many____

What is this character's mind set_____
_____
_____
_____

Immediate Family Members.
Mother_____ Nationality _____ Religion _____ D.O.B ____
Father_____ Nationality_____ Religion _____ D.O.B ____
Brothers_____, _____, _____

Sisters _____, _____, _____

Additional notes about this character:_____
_____
_____
_____
_____
_____
_____
_____
_____
_____
_____
_____
_____
_____
_____
_____
_____

Extended Family Members: Uncles & Aunts _____

Cousins_____Grand Parents_____
_____   _____

Book_____ Series_____ Protagonist or Antagonists

Full Name_____

D.O.B_____ Age _____ Nationality_____

Home Town or City _____ State or Country_____

Astrological sign_____ Religion_____ Beliefs_____

Married__ Single__ .What celebrity does this character most resemble_____

Human__ Alien__ Dimensional being___ Animal____

Offspring_____ How many____

What is this character's mind set_____
_____
_____
_____

Immediate Family Members.
Mother_____ Nationality _____ Religion _____ D.O.B ____
Father_____ Nationality_____ Religion _____ D.O.B ____
Brothers_____, _____, _____

Sisters _____, _____, _____

Additional notes about this character:_____
_____
_____
_____
_____
_____
_____
_____
_____
_____
_____
_____
_____
_____
_____
_____
_____

Extended Family Members: Uncles & Aunts _____

Cousins_____Grand Parents_____
_____   _____

Book_____ Series_____ Protagonist or Antagonists

Full Name_____

D.O.B_____ Age _____ Nationality_____

Home Town or City _____ State or Country_____

Astrological sign_____ Religion_____ Beliefs_____

Married__ Single__ _What celebrity does this character most resemble_____

Human__ Alien__ Dimensional being___ Animal____

Offspring_____ How many____

What is this character's mind set_____
_____
_____
_____

Immediate Family Members.
Mother_____ Nationality _____ Religion _____ D.O.B ____
Father_____ Nationality_____ Religion _____ D.O.B ____
Brothers_____, _____, _____

Sisters _____, _____, _____

Additional notes about this character:_____
_____
_____
_____
_____
_____
_____
_____
_____
_____
_____
_____
_____
_____
_____
_____
_____
_____

Extended Family Members: Uncles & Aunts _____

Cousins_____Grand Parents_____
_____   _____

Book_____ Series_____ Protagonist or Antagonists

Full Name_____

D.O.B_____ Age _____ Nationality_____

Home Town or City _____ State or Country_____

Astrological sign_____ Religion_____ Beliefs_____

Married__ Single__ _What celebrity does this character most resemble_____

Human__ Alien__ Dimensional being___ Animal_____

Offspring_____ How many_____

What is this character's mind set_____
_____
_____
_____

Immediate Family Members.
Mother_____ Nationality _____ Religion _____ D.O.B ____
Father_____ Nationality_____ Religion _____ D.O.B ____
Brothers_____, _____, _____

Sisters _____, _____, _____

Additional notes about this character:_____
_____
_____
_____
_____
_____
_____
_____
_____
_____
_____
_____
_____
_____
_____
_____
_____
_____
_____

Extended Family Members: Uncles & Aunts _____

Cousins_____Grand Parents_____
_____   _____

Book_____ Series_____ Protagonist or Antagonists

Full Name_____

D.O.B_____ Age _____ Nationality_____

Home Town or City _____ State or Country_____

Astrological sign_____ Religion_____ Beliefs_____

Married__ Single__ _What celebrity does this character most resemble_____

Human__ Alien__ Dimensional being___ Animal____

Offspring_____ How many____

What is this character's mind set_____
_____
_____
_____

Immediate Family Members.
Mother_____ Nationality _____ Religion _____ D.O.B ____
Father_____ Nationality_____ Religion _____ D.O.B ____
Brothers_____, _____, _____

Sisters _____, _____, _____

Additional notes about this character:_____
_____
_____
_____
_____
_____
_____
_____
_____
_____
_____
_____
_____
_____
_____
_____
_____
_____

Extended Family Members: Uncles & Aunts _____

Cousins_____Grand Parents_____
_____   _____

Book_____ Series_____ Protagonist or Antagonists

Full Name_____

D.O.B_____ Age _____ Nationality_____

Home Town or City _____ State or Country_____

Astrological sign_____ Religion_____ Beliefs_____

Married__ Single__ _What celebrity does this character most resemble_____

Human__ Alien__ Dimensional being___ Animal_____

Offspring_____ How many_____

What is this character's mind set_____
_____
_____
_____

Immediate Family Members.
Mother_____ Nationality _____ Religion _____ D.O.B ____
Father_____ Nationality_____ Religion _____ D.O.B ____
Brothers_____, _____, _____

Sisters _____, _____, _____

Additional notes about this character:_____
_____
_____
_____
_____
_____
_____
_____
_____
_____
_____
_____
_____
_____
_____
_____
_____
_____

Extended Family Members: Uncles & Aunts _____

Cousins_____Grand Parents_____
_____   _____

Book_____ Series_____ Protagonist or Antagonists

Full Name_____

D.O.B_____ Age _____ Nationality_____

Home Town or City _____ State or Country_____

Astrological sign_____ Religion_____ Beliefs_____

Married__ Single__ .What celebrity does this character most resemble_____

Human__ Alien__ Dimensional being___ Animal_____

Offspring_____ How many_____

What is this character's mind set_____
_____
_____
_____

Immediate Family Members.
Mother_____ Nationality _____ Religion _____ D.O.B ____
Father_____ Nationality_____ Religion _____ D.O.B ____
Brothers_____, _____, _____

Sisters _____, _____, _____

Additional notes about this character:_____
_____
_____
_____
_____
_____
_____
_____
_____
_____
_____
_____
_____
_____
_____
_____
_____
_____

Extended Family Members: Uncles & Aunts _____

Cousins_____Grand Parents_____
_____   _____

Book_____ Series_____ Protagonist or Antagonists

Full Name_____

D.O.B_____ Age _____ Nationality_____

Home Town or City _____ State or Country_____

Astrological sign_____ Religion_____ Beliefs_____

Married__ Single__ .What celebrity does this character most resemble_____

Human__ Alien__ Dimensional being___ Animal____

Offspring_____ How many____

What is this character's mind set_____
_____
_____
_____

Immediate Family Members.
Mother_____ Nationality _____ Religion _____ D.O.B ____
Father_____ Nationality_____ Religion _____ D.O.B ____
Brothers_____, _____, _____

Sisters _____, _____, _____

Additional notes about this character:_____
_____
_____
_____
_____
_____
_____
_____
_____
_____
_____
_____
_____
_____
_____
_____
_____
_____
_____

Extended Family Members: Uncles & Aunts _____

Cousins_____Grand Parents_____
_____   _____

Book_____ Series_____ Protagonist or Antagonists

Full Name_____

D.O.B_____ Age _____ Nationality_____

Home Town or City _____ State or Country_____

Astrological sign_____ Religion_____ Beliefs_____

Married__ Single__ _What celebrity does this character most resemble_____

Human__ Alien__ Dimensional being___ Animal_____

Offspring_____ How many_____

What is this character's mind set_____
_____
_____
_____

Immediate Family Members.
Mother_____ Nationality _____ Religion _____ D.O.B ____
Father_____ Nationality_____ Religion _____ D.O.B ____
Brothers_____, _____, _____

Sisters _____, _____, _____

Additional notes about this character:_____
_____
_____
_____
_____
_____
_____
_____
_____
_____
_____
_____
_____
_____
_____
_____
_____

Extended Family Members: Uncles & Aunts _____

Cousins_____Grand Parents_____
_____   _____

Book_____ Series_____ Protagonist or Antagonists

Full Name_____

D.O.B_____ Age _____ Nationality_____

Home Town or City _____ State or Country_____

Astrological sign_____ Religion_____ Beliefs_____

Married__ Single__ .What celebrity does this character most resemble_____

Human__ Alien__ Dimensional being___ Animal_____

Offspring_____ How many_____

What is this character's mind set_____
_____
_____
_____

Immediate Family Members.
Mother_____ Nationality _____ Religion _____ D.O.B ____
Father_____ Nationality_____ Religion _____ D.O.B ____
Brothers_____, _____, _____

Sisters _____, _____, _____

Additional notes about this character:_____
_____
_____
_____
_____
_____
_____
_____
_____
_____
_____
_____
_____
_____
_____
_____

Extended Family Members: Uncles & Aunts _____

Cousins_____Grand Parents_____
_____   _____

Book_____ Series_____ Protagonist or Antagonists

Full Name_____

D.O.B_____ Age _____ Nationality_____

Home Town or City _____ State or Country_____

Astrological sign_____ Religion_____ Beliefs_____

Married__ Single__ _What celebrity does this character most resemble_____

Human__ Alien__ Dimensional being___ Animal____

Offspring_____ How many____

What is this character's mind set_____
_____
_____
_____

Immediate Family Members.
Mother_____ Nationality _____ Religion _____ D.O.B ____
Father_____ Nationality_____ Religion _____ D.O.B ____
Brothers_____, _____, _____

Sisters _____, _____, _____

Additional notes about this character:_____
_____
_____
_____
_____
_____
_____
_____
_____
_____
_____
_____
_____
_____
_____
_____
_____
_____

Extended Family Members: Uncles & Aunts _____

Cousins_____Grand Parents_____
_____   _____

Book_____ Series_____ Protagonist or Antagonists

Full Name_____

D.O.B_____ Age _____ Nationality_____

Home Town or City _____ State or Country_____

Astrological sign_____ Religion_____ Beliefs_____

Married__ Single__ _What celebrity does this character most resemble_____

Human__ Alien__ Dimensional being___ Animal_____

Offspring_____ How many_____

What is this character's mind set_____
_____
_____
_____

Immediate Family Members.
Mother_____ Nationality _____ Religion _____ D.O.B ____
Father_____ Nationality_____ Religion _____ D.O.B ____
Brothers_____, _____, _____

Sisters _____, _____, _____

Additional notes about this character:_____
_____
_____
_____
_____
_____
_____
_____
_____
_____
_____
_____
_____
_____
_____
_____
_____
_____

Extended Family Members: Uncles & Aunts _____

Cousins_____Grand Parents_____
_____   _____

Book_____ Series_____ Protagonist or Antagonists

Full Name_____

D.O.B_____ Age _____ Nationality_____

Home Town or City _____ State or Country_____

Astrological sign_____ Religion_____ Beliefs_____

Married__ Single__ _What celebrity does this character most resemble_____

Human__ Alien__ Dimensional being___ Animal____

Offspring_____ How many____

What is this character's mind set_____
_____
_____
_____

Immediate Family Members.
Mother_____ Nationality _____ Religion _____ D.O.B ____
Father_____ Nationality_____ Religion _____ D.O.B ____
Brothers_____, _____, _____

Sisters _____, _____, _____

Additional notes about this character:_____
_____
_____
_____
_____
_____
_____
_____
_____
_____
_____
_____
_____
_____
_____
_____
_____
_____

Extended Family Members: Uncles & Aunts _____

Cousins_____Grand Parents_____
_____   _____

Book_____ Series_____ Protagonist or Antagonists

Full Name_____

D.O.B_____ Age _____ Nationality_____

Home Town or City _____ State or Country_____

Astrological sign_____ Religion_____ Beliefs_____

Married__ Single__ .What celebrity does this character most resemble_____

Human__ Alien__ Dimensional being___ Animal_____

Offspring_____ How many_____

What is this character's mind set_____
_____
_____
_____

Immediate Family Members.
Mother_____ Nationality _____ Religion _____ D.O.B ____
Father_____ Nationality_____ Religion _____ D.O.B ____
Brothers_____, _____, _____

Sisters _____, _____, _____

Additional notes about this character:_____
_____
_____
_____
_____
_____
_____
_____
_____
_____
_____
_____
_____
_____
_____
_____
_____

Extended Family Members: Uncles & Aunts _____

Cousins_____Grand Parents_____
_____   _____

Book_____ Series_____ Protagonist or Antagonists

Full Name_____

D.O.B_____ Age _____ Nationality_____

Home Town or City _____ State or Country_____

Astrological sign_____ Religion_____ Beliefs_____

Married__ Single__ _What celebrity does this character most resemble_____

Human__ Alien__ Dimensional being___ Animal____

Offspring_____ How many____

What is this character's mind set_____
_____
_____
_____

Immediate Family Members.
Mother_____ Nationality _____ Religion _____ D.O.B ____
Father_____ Nationality_____ Religion _____ D.O.B ____
Brothers_____, _____, _____

Sisters _____, _____, _____

Additional notes about this character:_____
_____
_____
_____
_____
_____
_____
_____
_____
_____
_____
_____
_____
_____
_____
_____
_____
_____

Extended Family Members: Uncles & Aunts _____

Cousins_____Grand Parents_____
_____   _____

Book_____ Series_____ Protagonist or Antagonists

Full Name_____

D.O.B_____ Age _____ Nationality_____

Home Town or City _____ State or Country_____

Astrological sign_____ Religion_____ Beliefs_____

Married__ Single__ _What celebrity does this character most resemble_____

Human__ Alien__ Dimensional being___ Animal_____

Offspring_____ How many_____

What is this character's mind set_____
_____
_____
_____

Immediate Family Members.
Mother_____ Nationality _____ Religion _____ D.O.B ____
Father_____ Nationality_____ Religion _____ D.O.B ____
Brothers_____, _____, _____

Sisters _____, _____, _____

Additional notes about this character:_____
_____
_____
_____
_____
_____
_____
_____
_____
_____
_____
_____
_____
_____
_____
_____
_____
_____

Extended Family Members: Uncles & Aunts _____

Cousins_____Grand Parents_____
_____   _____

Book_____ Series_____ Protagonist or Antagonists

Full Name_____

D.O.B_____ Age _____ Nationality_____

Home Town or City _____ State or Country_____

Astrological sign_____ Religion_____ Beliefs_____

Married__ Single__ _What celebrity does this character most resemble_____

Human__ Alien__ Dimensional being____ Animal_____

Offspring_____ How many_____

What is this character's mind set_____
_____
_____
_____

Immediate Family Members.
Mother_____ Nationality _____ Religion _____ D.O.B _____
Father_____ Nationality_____ Religion _____ D.O.B _____
Brothers_____, _____, _____

Sisters _____, _____, _____

Additional notes about this character:_____
_____
_____
_____
_____
_____
_____
_____
_____
_____
_____
_____
_____
_____
_____
_____
_____

Extended Family Members: Uncles & Aunts _____

Cousins_____Grand Parents_____
_____   _____

Book_____ Series_____ Protagonist or Antagonists

Full Name_____

D.O.B_____ Age _____ Nationality_____

Home Town or City _____ State or Country_____

Astrological sign_____ Religion_____ Beliefs_____

Married__ Single__ _What celebrity does this character most resemble_____

Human__ Alien__ Dimensional being___ Animal____

Offspring_____ How many____

What is this character's mind set_____
_____
_____
_____

Immediate Family Members.
Mother_____ Nationality _____ Religion _____ D.O.B ____
Father_____ Nationality_____ Religion _____ D.O.B ____
Brothers_____, _____, _____

Sisters _____, _____, _____

Additional notes about this character:_____
_____
_____
_____
_____
_____
_____
_____
_____
_____
_____
_____
_____
_____
_____
_____
_____
_____

Extended Family Members: Uncles & Aunts _____

Cousins_____Grand Parents_____
_____   _____

Book_____ Series_____ Protagonist or Antagonists

Full Name_____

D.O.B_____ Age _____ Nationality_____

Home Town or City _____ State or Country_____

Astrological sign_____ Religion_____ Beliefs_____

Married__ Single__ _What celebrity does this character most resemble_____

Human__ Alien__ Dimensional being___ Animal____

Offspring_____ How many____

What is this character's mind set_____
_____
_____
_____

Immediate Family Members.
Mother_____ Nationality _____ Religion _____ D.O.B ____
Father_____ Nationality_____ Religion _____ D.O.B ____
Brothers_____, _____, _____

Sisters _____, _____, _____

Additional notes about this character:_____
_____
_____
_____
_____
_____
_____
_____
_____
_____
_____
_____
_____
_____
_____
_____
_____
_____

Extended Family Members: Uncles & Aunts _____

Cousins_____Grand Parents_____
_____   _____

Book_____ Series_____ Protagonist or Antagonists

Full Name_____

D.O.B_____ Age _____ Nationality_____

Home Town or City _____ State or Country_____

Astrological sign_____ Religion_____ Beliefs_____

Married__ Single__ .What celebrity does this character most resemble_____

Human__ Alien__ Dimensional being___ Animal_____

Offspring_____ How many_____

What is this character's mind set_____
_____
_____
_____

Immediate Family Members.
Mother_____ Nationality _____ Religion _____ D.O.B _____
Father_____ Nationality_____ Religion _____ D.O.B _____
Brothers_____, _____, _____

Sisters _____, _____, _____

Additional notes about this character:_____
_____
_____
_____
_____
_____
_____
_____
_____
_____
_____
_____
_____
_____
_____
_____
_____

Extended Family Members: Uncles & Aunts _____

Cousins_____Grand Parents_____
_____   _____

Book_____ Series_____ Protagonist or Antagonists

Full Name_____

D.O.B_____ Age _____ Nationality_____

Home Town or City _____ State or Country_____

Astrological sign_____ Religion_____ Beliefs_____

Married__ Single__ _What celebrity does this character most resemble_____

Human__ Alien__ Dimensional being___ Animal_____

Offspring_____ How many_____

What is this character's mind set_____
_____
_____
_____

Immediate Family Members.
Mother_____ Nationality _____ Religion _____ D.O.B _____
Father_____ Nationality_____ Religion _____ D.O.B _____
Brothers_____, _____, _____

Sisters _____, _____, _____

Additional notes about this character:_____
_____
_____
_____
_____
_____
_____
_____
_____
_____
_____
_____
_____
_____
_____
_____

Extended Family Members: Uncles & Aunts _____

Cousins_____Grand Parents_____
_____   _____

Book_____ Series_____ Protagonist or Antagonists

Full Name_____

D.O.B_____ Age _____ Nationality_____

Home Town or City _____ State or Country_____

Astrological sign_____ Religion_____ Beliefs_____

Married__ Single__ _What celebrity does this character most resemble_____

Human__ Alien__ Dimensional being___ Animal____

Offspring_____ How many____

What is this character's mind set_____
_____
_____
_____

Immediate Family Members.
Mother_____ Nationality _____ Religion _____ D.O.B ____
Father_____ Nationality_____ Religion _____ D.O.B ____
Brothers_____, _____, _____

Sisters _____, _____, _____

Additional notes about this character:_____
_____
_____
_____
_____
_____
_____
_____
_____
_____
_____
_____
_____
_____
_____
_____
_____
_____

Extended Family Members: Uncles & Aunts _____

Cousins_____Grand Parents_____
_____   _____

Book_____ Series_____ Protagonist or Antagonists

Full Name_____

D.O.B_____ Age _____ Nationality_____

Home Town or City _____ State or Country_____

Astrological sign_____ Religion_____ Beliefs_____

Married___ Single___ _What celebrity does this character most resemble_____

Human___ Alien___ Dimensional being____ Animal_____

Offspring_____ How many_____

What is this character's mind set_____
_____
_____
_____
_____

Immediate Family Members.
Mother_____ Nationality _____ Religion _____ D.O.B ____
Father_____ Nationality_____ Religion _____ D.O.B ____
Brothers_____, _____, _____

Sisters _____, _____, _____

Additional notes about this character:_____
_____
_____
_____
_____
_____
_____
_____
_____
_____
_____
_____
_____
_____
_____
_____
_____

Extended Family Members: Uncles & Aunts _____

Cousins_____Grand Parents_____
_____   _____

Book_____ Series_____ Protagonist or Antagonists

Full Name_____

D.O.B_____ Age _____ Nationality_____

Home Town or City _____ State or Country_____

Astrological sign_____ Religion_____ Beliefs_____

Married__ Single__ _What celebrity does this character most resemble_____

Human__ Alien__ Dimensional being___ Animal____

Offspring_____ How many____

What is this character's mind set_____
_____
_____
_____

Immediate Family Members.
Mother_____ Nationality _____ Religion _____ D.O.B ____
Father_____ Nationality_____ Religion _____ D.O.B ____
Brothers_____, _____, _____

Sisters _____, _____, _____

Additional notes about this character:_____
_____
_____
_____
_____
_____
_____
_____
_____
_____
_____
_____
_____
_____
_____
_____
_____

Extended Family Members: Uncles & Aunts _____

Cousins_____Grand Parents_____
_____   _____

Book_____ Series_____ Protagonist or Antagonists

Full Name_____

D.O.B_____ Age _____ Nationality_____

Home Town or City _____ State or Country_____

Astrological sign_____ Religion_____ Beliefs_____

Married__ Single__ _What celebrity does this character most resemble_____

Human__ Alien__ Dimensional being___ Animal_____

Offspring_____ How many____

What is this character's mind set_____
_____
_____
_____

Immediate Family Members.
Mother_____ Nationality _____ Religion _____ D.O.B ____
Father_____ Nationality_____ Religion _____ D.O.B ____
Brothers_____, _____, _____

Sisters _____, _____, _____

Additional notes about this character:_____
_____
_____
_____
_____
_____
_____
_____
_____
_____
_____
_____
_____
_____
_____
_____
_____
_____

Extended Family Members: Uncles & Aunts _____

Cousins_____Grand Parents_____
_____   _____

Book_____ Series_____ Protagonist or Antagonists

Full Name_____

D.O.B_____ Age _____ Nationality_____

Home Town or City _____ State or Country_____

Astrological sign_____ Religion_____ Beliefs_____

Married__ Single__ _What celebrity does this character most resemble_____

Human__ Alien__ Dimensional being____ Animal_____

Offspring_____ How many_____

What is this character's mind set_____
_____
_____
_____

Immediate Family Members.
Mother_____ Nationality _____ Religion _____ D.O.B ____
Father_____ Nationality_____ Religion _____ D.O.B ____
Brothers_____, _____, _____

Sisters _____, _____, _____

Additional notes about this character:_____
_____
_____
_____
_____
_____
_____
_____
_____
_____
_____
_____
_____
_____
_____
_____
_____
_____

Extended Family Members: Uncles & Aunts _____

Cousins_____Grand Parents_____
_____   _____

Book_____ Series_____ Protagonist or Antagonists

Full Name_____

D.O.B_____ Age _____ Nationality_____

Home Town or City _____ State or Country_____

Astrological sign_____ Religion_____ Beliefs_____

Married__ Single__ What celebrity does this character most resemble_____

Human__ Alien__ Dimensional being___ Animal____

Offspring_____ How many____

What is this character's mind set_____
_____
_____
_____

Immediate Family Members.
Mother_____ Nationality _____ Religion _____ D.O.B ____
Father_____ Nationality_____ Religion _____ D.O.B ____
Brothers_____, _____, _____

Sisters _____, _____, _____

Additional notes about this character:_____
_____
_____
_____
_____
_____
_____
_____
_____
_____
_____
_____
_____
_____
_____
_____
_____
_____

Extended Family Members: Uncles & Aunts _____

Cousins_____Grand Parents_____
_____   _____

Book_____ Series_____ Protagonist or Antagonists

Full Name_____

D.O.B_____ Age _____ Nationality_____

Home Town or City _____ State or Country_____

Astrological sign_____ Religion_____ Beliefs_____

Married__ Single__ _What celebrity does this character most resemble_____

Human__ Alien__ Dimensional being___ Animal____

Offspring_____ How many____

What is this character's mind set_____
_____
_____
_____

Immediate Family Members.
Mother_____ Nationality _____ Religion _____ D.O.B ____
Father_____ Nationality_____ Religion _____ D.O.B ____
Brothers_____, _____, _____

Sisters _____, _____, _____

Additional notes about this character:_____
_____
_____
_____
_____
_____
_____
_____
_____
_____
_____
_____
_____
_____
_____
_____
_____
_____

Extended Family Members: Uncles & Aunts _____

Cousins_____Grand Parents_____
_____   _____

Book_____ Series_____ Protagonist or Antagonists

Full Name_____

D.O.B_____ Age _____ Nationality_____

Home Town or City _____ State or Country_____

Astrological sign_____ Religion_____ Beliefs_____

Married___ Single___ .What celebrity does this character most resemble_____

Human___ Alien___ Dimensional being____ Animal_____

Offspring_____ How many_____

What is this character's mind set_____
_____
_____
_____

Immediate Family Members.
Mother_____ Nationality _____ Religion _____ D.O.B ____
Father_____ Nationality_____ Religion _____ D.O.B ____
Brothers_____, _____, _____

Sisters _____, _____, _____

Additional notes about this character:_____
_____
_____
_____
_____
_____
_____
_____
_____
_____
_____
_____
_____
_____
_____
_____
_____
_____

Extended Family Members: Uncles & Aunts _____

Cousins_____Grand Parents_____
_____   _____

Book_____ Series_____ Protagonist or Antagonists

Full Name_____

D.O.B_____ Age _____ Nationality_____

Home Town or City _____ State or Country_____

Astrological sign_____ Religion_____ Beliefs_____

Married__ Single__ _What celebrity does this character most resemble_____

Human__ Alien__ Dimensional being___ Animal_____

Offspring_____ How many_____

What is this character's mind set_____
_____
_____
_____

Immediate Family Members.
Mother_____ Nationality _____ Religion _____ D.O.B ____
Father_____ Nationality_____ Religion _____ D.O.B ____
Brothers_____, _____, _____

Sisters _____, _____, _____

Additional notes about this character:_____
_____
_____
_____
_____
_____
_____
_____
_____
_____
_____
_____
_____
_____
_____
_____
_____
_____

Extended Family Members: Uncles & Aunts _____

Cousins_____Grand Parents_____
_____   _____

Book_____ Series_____ Protagonist or Antagonists

Full Name_____

D.O.B_____ Age _____ Nationality_____

Home Town or City _____ State or Country_____

Astrological sign_____ Religion_____ Beliefs_____

Married__ Single__ .What celebrity does this character most resemble_____

Human__ Alien__ Dimensional being___ Animal_____

Offspring_____ How many_____

What is this character's mind set_____
_____
_____
_____

Immediate Family Members.
Mother_____ Nationality _____ Religion _____ D.O.B _____
Father_____ Nationality_____ Religion _____ D.O.B _____
Brothers_____, _____, _____

Sisters _____, _____, _____

Additional notes about this character:_____
_____
_____
_____
_____
_____
_____
_____
_____
_____
_____
_____
_____
_____
_____
_____
_____
_____

Extended Family Members: Uncles & Aunts _____

Cousins_____Grand Parents_____
_____   _____

Book_____ Series_____ Protagonist or Antagonists

Full Name_____

D.O.B_____ Age _____ Nationality_____

Home Town or City _____ State or Country_____

Astrological sign_____ Religion_____ Beliefs_____

Married__ Single__ _What celebrity does this character most resemble_____

Human__ Alien__ Dimensional being___ Animal____

Offspring_____ How many____

What is this character's mind set_____
_____
_____
_____

Immediate Family Members.
Mother_____ Nationality _____ Religion _____ D.O.B ____
Father_____ Nationality_____ Religion _____ D.O.B ____
Brothers_____, _____, _____

Sisters _____, _____, _____

Additional notes about this character:_____
_____
_____
_____
_____
_____
_____
_____
_____
_____
_____
_____
_____
_____
_____
_____
_____
_____

Extended Family Members: Uncles & Aunts _____

Cousins_____Grand Parents_____
_____   _____

Book_____ Series_____ Protagonist or Antagonists

Full Name_____

D.O.B_____ Age _____ Nationality_____

Home Town or City _____ State or Country_____

Astrological sign_____ Religion_____ Beliefs_____

Married__ Single__ _What celebrity does this character most resemble_____

Human__ Alien__ Dimensional being___ Animal_____

Offspring_____ How many_____

What is this character's mind set_____
_____
_____
_____

Immediate Family Members.
Mother_____ Nationality _____ Religion _____ D.O.B ____
Father_____ Nationality_____ Religion _____ D.O.B ____
Brothers_____, _____, _____

Sisters _____, _____, _____

Additional notes about this character:_____
_____
_____
_____
_____
_____
_____
_____
_____
_____
_____
_____
_____
_____
_____
_____
_____
_____

Extended Family Members: Uncles & Aunts _____

Cousins_____Grand Parents_____
_____   _____

Book_____ Series_____ Protagonist or Antagonists

Full Name_____

D.O.B_____ Age _____ Nationality_____

Home Town or City _____ State or Country_____

Astrological sign_____ Religion_____ Beliefs_____

Married__ Single___ _What celebrity does this character most resemble_____

Human__ Alien__ Dimensional being___ Animal_____

Offspring_____ How many_____

What is this character's mind set_____
_____
_____
_____

Immediate Family Members.
Mother_____ Nationality _____ Religion _____ D.O.B ____
Father_____ Nationality_____ Religion _____ D.O.B ____
Brothers_____, _____, _____

Sisters _____, _____, _____

Additional notes about this character:_____
_____
_____
_____
_____
_____
_____
_____
_____
_____
_____
_____
_____
_____
_____
_____
_____
_____
_____

Extended Family Members: Uncles & Aunts _____

Cousins_____Grand Parents_____
_____   _____

Book_____ Series_____ Protagonist or Antagonists

Full Name_____

D.O.B_____ Age _____ Nationality_____

Home Town or City _____ State or Country_____

Astrological sign_____ Religion_____ Beliefs_____

Married__ Single__ .What celebrity does this character most resemble_____

Human__ Alien__ Dimensional being___ Animal____

Offspring_____ How many____

What is this character's mind set_____
_____
_____
_____

<u>Immediate Family Members.</u>
Mother_____ Nationality _____ Religion _____ D.O.B ____
Father_____ Nationality_____ Religion _____ D.O.B ____
Brothers_____, _____, _____

Sisters _____, _____, _____

Additional notes about this character:_____
_____
_____
_____
_____
_____
_____
_____
_____
_____
_____
_____
_____
_____
_____
_____
_____
_____

Extended Family Members: Uncles & Aunts _____

Cousins_____Grand Parents_____
_____   _____

Book_____ Series_____ Protagonist or Antagonists

Full Name_____

D.O.B_____ Age _____ Nationality_____

Home Town or City _____ State or Country_____

Astrological sign_____ Religion_____ Beliefs_____

Married__ Single__ _What celebrity does this character most resemble_____

Human__ Alien__ Dimensional being___ Animal____

Offspring_____ How many____

What is this character's mind set_____
_____
_____
_____

Immediate Family Members.
Mother_____ Nationality _____ Religion _____ D.O.B ____
Father_____ Nationality_____ Religion _____ D.O.B ____
Brothers_____, _____, _____

Sisters _____, _____, _____

Additional notes about this character:_____
_____
_____
_____
_____
_____
_____
_____
_____
_____
_____
_____
_____
_____
_____
_____
_____

Extended Family Members: Uncles & Aunts _____

Cousins_____Grand Parents_____
_____   _____

Book_____ Series_____ Protagonist or Antagonists

Full Name_____

D.O.B_____ Age _____ Nationality_____

Home Town or City _____ State or Country_____

Astrological sign_____ Religion_____ Beliefs_____

Married__ Single__ _What celebrity does this character most resemble_____

Human__ Alien__ Dimensional being____ Animal_____

Offspring_____ How many_____

What is this character's mind set_____
_____
_____
_____

Immediate Family Members.
Mother_____ Nationality _____ Religion _____ D.O.B ____
Father_____ Nationality_____ Religion _____ D.O.B ____
Brothers_____, _____, _____

Sisters _____, _____, _____

Additional notes about this character:_____
_____
_____
_____
_____
_____
_____
_____
_____
_____
_____
_____
_____
_____
_____
_____
_____
_____

Extended Family Members: Uncles & Aunts _____

Cousins_____Grand Parents_____
_____   _____

Book_____ Series_____ Protagonist or Antagonists

Full Name_____

D.O.B_____ Age _____ Nationality_____

Home Town or City _____ State or Country_____

Astrological sign_____ Religion_____ Beliefs_____

Married__ Single__ .What celebrity does this character most resemble_____

Human__ Alien__ Dimensional being___ Animal_____

Offspring_____ How many_____

What is this character's mind set_____
_____
_____
_____

Immediate Family Members.
Mother_____ Nationality _____ Religion _____ D.O.B ____
Father_____ Nationality_____ Religion _____ D.O.B ____
Brothers_____, _____, _____

Sisters _____, _____, _____

Additional notes about this character:_____
_____
_____
_____
_____
_____
_____
_____
_____
_____
_____
_____
_____
_____
_____
_____
_____
_____

Extended Family Members: Uncles & Aunts _____

Cousins_____Grand Parents_____
_____   _____

Book_____ Series_____ Protagonist or Antagonists

Full Name_____

D.O.B_____ Age _____ Nationality_____

Home Town or City _____ State or Country_____

Astrological sign_____ Religion_____ Beliefs_____

Married__ Single__ .What celebrity does this character most resemble_____

Human__ Alien__ Dimensional being___ Animal_____

Offspring_____ How many_____

What is this character's mind set_____
_____
_____
_____

Immediate Family Members.
Mother_____ Nationality _____ Religion _____ D.O.B ____
Father_____ Nationality_____ Religion _____ D.O.B ____
Brothers_____, _____, _____

Sisters _____, _____, _____

Additional notes about this character:_____
_____
_____
_____
_____
_____
_____
_____
_____
_____
_____
_____
_____
_____
_____
_____
_____
_____

Extended Family Members: Uncles & Aunts _____

Cousins_____Grand Parents_____
_____   _____

Book_____ Series_____ Protagonist or Antagonists

Full Name_____

D.O.B_____ Age _____ Nationality_____

Home Town or City _____ State or Country_____

Astrological sign_____ Religion_____ Beliefs_____

Married__ Single__ _What celebrity does this character most resemble_____

Human__ Alien__ Dimensional being___ Animal____

Offspring_____ How many____

What is this character's mind set_____
_____
_____
_____

Immediate Family Members.
Mother_____ Nationality _____ Religion _____ D.O.B ____
Father_____ Nationality_____ Religion _____ D.O.B ____
Brothers_____, _____, _____

Sisters _____, _____, _____

Additional notes about this character:_____
_____
_____
_____
_____
_____
_____
_____
_____
_____
_____
_____
_____
_____
_____
_____
_____
_____

Extended Family Members: Uncles & Aunts _____

Cousins_____Grand Parents_____
_____   _____

Book_____ Series_____ Protagonist or Antagonists

Full Name_____

D.O.B_____ Age _____ Nationality_____

Home Town or City _____ State or Country_____

Astrological sign_____ Religion_____ Beliefs_____

Married__ Single__ _What celebrity does this character most resemble_____

Human__ Alien__ Dimensional being___ Animal____

Offspring_____ How many____

What is this character's mind set_____
_____
_____
_____

Immediate Family Members.
Mother_____ Nationality _____ Religion _____ D.O.B ____
Father_____ Nationality_____ Religion _____ D.O.B ____
Brothers_____, _____, _____

Sisters _____, _____, _____

Additional notes about this character:_____
_____
_____
_____
_____
_____
_____
_____
_____
_____
_____
_____
_____
_____
_____
_____
_____
_____

Extended Family Members: Uncles & Aunts _____

Cousins_____Grand Parents_____
_____   _____

Book_____ Series_____ Protagonist or Antagonists

Full Name_____

D.O.B_____ Age _____ Nationality_____

Home Town or City _____ State or Country_____

Astrological sign_____ Religion_____ Beliefs_____

Married__ Single__ _What celebrity does this character most resemble_____

Human__ Alien__ Dimensional being___ Animal_____

Offspring_____ How many_____

What is this character's mind set_____
_____
_____
_____

Immediate Family Members.
Mother_____ Nationality _____ Religion _____ D.O.B _____
Father_____ Nationality_____ Religion _____ D.O.B _____
Brothers_____, _____, _____

Sisters _____, _____, _____

Additional notes about this character:_____
_____
_____
_____
_____
_____
_____
_____
_____
_____
_____
_____
_____
_____
_____
_____
_____
_____
_____

Extended Family Members: Uncles & Aunts _____

Cousins_____Grand Parents_____
_____   _____

Book_____ Series_____ Protagonist or Antagonists

Full Name_____

D.O.B_____ Age _____ Nationality_____

Home Town or City _____ State or Country_____

Astrological sign_____ Religion_____ Beliefs_____

Married___ Single___ .What celebrity does this character most resemble_____

Human___ Alien___ Dimensional being____ Animal_____

Offspring_____ How many_____

What is this character's mind set_____
_____
_____
_____

Immediate Family Members.
Mother_____ Nationality _____ Religion _____ D.O.B _____
Father_____ Nationality_____ Religion _____ D.O.B _____
Brothers_____, _____, _____

Sisters _____, _____, _____

Additional notes about this character:_____
_____
_____
_____
_____
_____
_____
_____
_____
_____
_____
_____
_____
_____
_____
_____
_____
_____
_____

Extended Family Members: Uncles & Aunts _____

Cousins_____Grand Parents_____
_____   _____

Book_____ Series_____ Protagonist or Antagonists

Full Name_____

D.O.B_____ Age _____ Nationality_____

Home Town or City _____ State or Country_____

Astrological sign_____ Religion_____ Beliefs_____

Married__ Single__ _What celebrity does this character most resemble_____

Human__ Alien__ Dimensional being____ Animal_____

Offspring_____ How many_____

What is this character's mind set_____
_____
_____
_____

Immediate Family Members.
Mother_____ Nationality _____ Religion _____ D.O.B ____
Father_____ Nationality_____ Religion _____ D.O.B ____
Brothers_____, _____, _____

Sisters _____, _____, _____

Additional notes about this character:_____
_____
_____
_____
_____
_____
_____
_____
_____
_____
_____
_____
_____
_____
_____
_____
_____

Extended Family Members: Uncles & Aunts _____

Cousins_____Grand Parents_____
_____   _____

Book_____ Series_____ Protagonist or Antagonists

Full Name_____

D.O.B_____ Age _____ Nationality_____

Home Town or City _____ State or Country_____

Astrological sign_____ Religion_____ Beliefs_____

Married__ Single__ .What celebrity does this character most resemble_____

Human__ Alien__ Dimensional being___ Animal_____

Offspring_____ How many_____

What is this character's mind set_____
_____
_____
_____

Immediate Family Members.
Mother_____ Nationality _____ Religion _____ D.O.B ____
Father_____ Nationality_____ Religion _____ D.O.B ____
Brothers_____, _____, _____

Sisters _____, _____, _____

Additional notes about this character:_____
_____
_____
_____
_____
_____
_____
_____
_____
_____
_____
_____
_____
_____
_____
_____
_____
_____

Extended Family Members: Uncles & Aunts _____

Cousins_____Grand Parents_____
_____   _____

Book_____ Series_____ Protagonist or Antagonists

Full Name_____

D.O.B_____ Age _____ Nationality_____

Home Town or City _____ State or Country_____

Astrological sign_____ Religion_____ Beliefs_____

Married__ Single__ .What celebrity does this character most resemble_____

Human__ Alien__ Dimensional being___ Animal_____

Offspring_____ How many_____

What is this character's mind set_____
_____
_____
_____

Immediate Family Members.
Mother_____ Nationality _____ Religion _____ D.O.B ____
Father_____ Nationality_____ Religion _____ D.O.B ____
Brothers_____, _____, _____

Sisters _____, _____, _____

Additional notes about this character:_____
_____
_____
_____
_____
_____
_____
_____
_____
_____
_____
_____
_____
_____
_____
_____
_____
_____

Extended Family Members: Uncles & Aunts _____

Cousins_____Grand Parents_____
_____   _____

Book_____ Series_____ Protagonist or Antagonists

Full Name_____

D.O.B_____ Age _____ Nationality_____

Home Town or City _____ State or Country_____

Astrological sign_____ Religion_____ Beliefs_____

Married__ Single__ _What celebrity does this character most resemble_____

Human__ Alien__ Dimensional being___ Animal_____

Offspring_____ How many_____

What is this character's mind set_____
_____
_____
_____

<u>Immediate Family Members</u>.
Mother_____ Nationality _____ Religion _____ D.O.B ____
Father_____ Nationality_____ Religion _____ D.O.B ____
Brothers_____, _____, _____

Sisters _____, _____, _____

Additional notes about this character:_____
_____
_____
_____
_____
_____
_____
_____
_____
_____
_____
_____
_____
_____
_____
_____
_____
_____

Extended Family Members: Uncles & Aunts _____

Cousins_____Grand Parents_____
_____   _____

Book_____ Series_____ Protagonist or Antagonists

Full Name_____

D.O.B_____ Age _____ Nationality_____

Home Town or City _____ State or Country_____

Astrological sign_____ Religion_____ Beliefs_____

Married__ Single__ _What celebrity does this character most resemble_____

Human__ Alien__ Dimensional being___ Animal____

Offspring_____ How many____

What is this character's mind set_____
_____
_____
_____

Immediate Family Members.
Mother_____ Nationality _____ Religion _____ D.O.B ____
Father_____ Nationality_____ Religion _____ D.O.B ____
Brothers_____, _____, _____

Sisters _____, _____, _____

Additional notes about this character:_____
_____
_____
_____
_____
_____
_____
_____
_____
_____
_____
_____
_____
_____
_____
_____
_____

Extended Family Members: Uncles & Aunts _____

Cousins_____Grand Parents_____
_____   _____

Book_____ Series_____ Protagonist or Antagonists

Full Name_____

D.O.B_____ Age _____ Nationality_____

Home Town or City _____ State or Country_____

Astrological sign_____ Religion_____ Beliefs_____

Married___ Single___ _What celebrity does this character most resemble_____

Human___ Alien___ Dimensional being____ Animal_____

Offspring_____ How many_____

What is this character's mind set_____
_____
_____
_____

Immediate Family Members.
Mother_____ Nationality _____ Religion _____ D.O.B ____
Father_____ Nationality_____ Religion _____ D.O.B ____
Brothers_____, _____, _____

Sisters _____, _____, _____

Additional notes about this character:_____
_____
_____
_____
_____
_____
_____
_____
_____
_____
_____
_____
_____
_____
_____
_____
_____
_____
_____

Extended Family Members: Uncles & Aunts _____

Cousins_____Grand Parents_____
_____   _____